A Anna Terrana
Con viva stima e
simpatia

Diego
2015

The Bloody Thorn

Diego Bastianutti
2014

To Giusy,

"Being deeply loved by someone gives you strength, while loving someone deeply gives you courage."

Lao Tzu

Introduction to *The Bloody Thorn*

Giusy Cecilia Oddo

There is no doubt that this fourth collection of poems by Diego Bastianutti is all pure poetry. Its high tone is polished and unbroken; nothing is trite, discursive or superfluous. Every word, every verse, every image is essential to the perfect whole of the composition and to the intensity of its import. The poet goes even a step further in the true poetic creative process, that by which the rational content is urged towards the secret irrationality of the form, as the critic Stefano Agosti writes. In other words, an expression where the concept is not reached through reason but grasped through the power and the suggestion of the 'form,' of the image. So that to reveal does not mean to reduce the concept to intelligible terms. The conscious thought is thus enriched with multiple echoes and meanings, which is the real nature of poetry, aiming at the soul. The mystery of human existence, with its unanswered questions, its tragic irony, its loneliness is, for example, enclosed in the evocative, deeply meaningful metaphors of these few lines:

...blindly on the shore/ we peer each night into the silent/ scalloped pearl of the fog-shrouded sea/ and we gather all but fragments/ of vessels shattered at Creation/ bearing witness to a game of seduction/ as our masterminded god/ keeps teasing us to death", while the hopes of life rest on "*a promise of nirvana on*

the wing/ of crystal birds" (Crystal Birds). Clearly, the poet searches for and uses the mysterious, almost mystical value of the written word.

In spite of the anti-narrative tone, the poetic work of Bastianutti has a marked autobiographical character. The poet deals with the experience of leaving his mother-country, the forced exile, the search for his own identity denied just at the moment of its formation. This is followed by his becoming aware of the real world, of its injustices, and of the need to awaken the social consciousness; to force it with the lash of his word -his best instrument-, to "see" and not merely "to look". Then there are the poems that speak of the comfort which love has given him in the autumn of his well-tested life. Accordingly, the collection is divided in three well-balance sections, with some twenty poems each, reflecting the three principal phases of the poet's emotional and existential experience, without necessarily in a chronological order.

The collection tellingly opens with poems of social criticism, "The Bloody Thorn," the indignation at the ignorance, the indifference and the hypocrisy of our society being the main impetus in this first part of Bastianutti's collection. Hence, the intense verses laying bare the wounds of human misery, indeed "the bloody thorn," which are the uncomfortable bur as well, thrust by the poet into the apathy of mankind. The poet launches his battle with the weapon of the word, well conscious of its power, and he directs it against a world in which the word has been emptied of its true meaning, has been corrupted. Words like "democracy and freedom" which are "*dead words draped on gun barrels*" in a world where "*drunken gods are playing chess on our backs*" (For Just a While). "The word" is a recurrent theme throughout this part of the collection, in which the poet fights the falsehoods of the world, "*I'll rip to shreds the mask/ of words;*" while the "words" that he wants to use instead are the ones that give shape to "*those perfect pearly moons*" in which he wraps the thoughts he writes (Janus Moons). "C'est le monde de mots qui crée le monde de choses," as Lacan says.

With superbly incisive images of intense insight, creating metaphorical exchanges between myth and reality, the poet conjures up "*the silent scream of men,*" of soldiers who died for "*gleaming crosses,*" on generals' chests, while women dream of a day when they will not have to give birth to men condemned to death, and they scan "*the world's edge/ for Ariadne's saving thread/ to end the endless craving/ of the Minotaur in us*" (The Last to Die). He warns us against a society in which "*we are taught how to compute/ not to think,*" relying on a progress which is in "*the hands of souls devoid of humanity*" (Future Perfect). In the poem "Fahrenheit 451, Bastianutti echoes Heinrich Heine's 1821 prophetic message, "Where they burn books, so too will they in the end burn human beings," by adding his own sharp reminder, "*When a book burns/ man's very soul/ is murdered."*

From considerations of the world at large, the poet narrows his focus on the microcosm of his own city. He moves from the threat of collective social self-destruction to the *de facto,* not always deliberate, drug-induced personal self-destruction - *"the needle bites into the cursing blood/ trading all for utter void/ floating in a womb/ of lethal fluid/ the mind a dry desert dune/ sucking all thought/ gone all pain/ grief/ guilt/shame/ desire"* -(Romancing the Stone); to that caused by poverty – *"I've seen the ancient pride/ of first nation/ bent over/ picking butts to stich/ them whole for trade/ oh yeah"* – (I've seen....); and then to the urban blight *"in Vancouver's own favelas."* Thus, Bastianutti gives a powerful picture of a painful and very human social scene, so much ignored, of the injustice he wants to denounce till his last breath, *"I won't go quietly/ into the night,"* echoing Dylan Thomas.

This section of the book closes with a symbol of hoped-for innocence represented by the poem dedicated to Vancouver's Wreck Beach, an Eden-like site, while the poet hopes to find again his childhood innocence, so that *"I might look/ into my grandchild's/ sky-blue eyes/ with a promise of spring"* (For Just a While).

The second part of the collection, "Love After Dusk," is dedicated to love and to woman. To the evil decried in the first part, the poet opposes Psyche, that is the feminine soul which merges with Eros in a union made of grief and catharsis, *"raise me/ from all that's foul/ wash the sting of evil seen/ from my eyes/ carve me/ with your desire/ that I might feel/ the constant/ scar of love"* (Scar).

That incessant almost obsessive search for the feminine essence, that elusive mystery which the deeper we delve in the more it escapes us - is the main theme of the assorted group of poems, in which woman is shown in her various facets: the caring woman, the life-giving woman, the nurturing woman, the enigma woman, the woman lover, the woman victim, the woman wrapped in her ancient silence. This complex portrait reaches its culmination in the splendid long work -almost an epic poem- "Penelope." In its verses - with echoes as ancient, mysterious and mythical as woman herself - all the notes which represent her are subsumed and merged in a powerful symphony. The feminine mystery becomes one with the mystery of our very existence.

"All seems to be key to another mystery/ never to the mystery itself./ But perhaps the mystery is in her/ within this tiny frail woman/ her beauty as fine as her bones now/ thin as the edge of a blade."

From woman in general, the poet enters the realm of personal experience, the woman loved, no less elusive in her mystery - her *"unfinished nature/ a metaphor veiled in flesh"* (Love After Dusk). To this woman he dedicates beautiful verses of a delicate sensuality, *"the silvery fascia winding/ round the rising hip I trace/ with fevered fingers,"* and lyricism, *"I want to slow the streak of stars/ the lunar flashing curve/ in the night sky/ my love"* (I want).

The last poem "Love After Dusk," which closes the journey across the engaging feminine "enigma," finds the poet still groping in the dark, trying to grasp his Psyche, akin to the mythical soul-hungry owl - *"He moves in Stygian darkness/ groping like an owl for a soul/ to consume her fleeting shadow."* His entire existence is a feeding off shadows in the darkness of a dubious reality; his only sanctuary is to hold on to the gaze of her loving eyes, *"an ancient wind presses/ against our tangled shadows/ I hold your eyes,"* knowing though that she too is *"purely in loan"* to him.

I wholly agree with the critic Egidio Marchese who, referring to this poem says, "Intense and concise expression, particularly extraordinary in this poem, as in all the spellbinding poetry of Diego Bastianutti."

The poems that close this collection are the most explicitly autobiographical. The memory theme, the return to his childhood, the drama of the exodus and of emigration, of the disconnection between two worlds alternate with reflections on life and death, on the passing of time.

The protagonist of this third section is the *"Antevasin,"* a word that in Sanskrit refers to a border-dweller, that is a man in between two countries, and without a homeland, with whom Bastianutti identifies. And it means as well "a scholar who lives in the sight of two worlds, but is looking towards the unknown," which is an appropriate definition for Diego Bastianutti, a scholar who is enriched by the perspectives and the culture of two worlds, and always open towards new horizons.

The balanced maturity is reached only after a long anguished process, after a hard-won inner battle. First of all the trauma of his uprooting, as a child, from a 'land' that was 'mother' - the exodus, first from the *Giuliano-Dalmati* territories and then from Italy itself, losing in the process his own identity. Hence the poems dealing mainly with the quest for the lost self, "*I am the world/ in which I walk/ displaced from my homeland/ as much as from myself?*" (Twice Displaced). Fiume, the historic, independent city - it too compelled to change its name, its identity, becoming the Croatian Rijeka - remains his "beloved albatross", "*...I cannot let go/ the one ghost-feather/ my fingers keep brushing – Fiume- /I still hear her calling out to me*"(Beloved Albatross). His birthplace was as well the land of his innocent years, an innocence now lost, which can be regained only if he is able to let go of the memory of that past, "*my innocence was redeemed/ by a five-year long amnesia/ that with the rubble /had swept away a past as well / that had bloomed in me/ yet bore no fruit*" (The Class of '39). That land, that past twice lost were not able to contribute in forging the man. Quite a different impact was waiting for him on his arrival in the "new world," the essence of which is summed up by the poet in "The Impossible

Equation." The poem leaves a powerful impression in this final part of the book, where the poet voices in a concise, poignant cry the trampled human dignity experienced by him on his arrival in the Unites States, which opened him its doors on the Mississippi River. The sight of the children on his own ship being thrown discarded fruit fused symbolically with the sight of American blacks swimming in the river's muddy waters to grab the food waste left in the wake of the ship.

Through these painful experiences, the *Antevasin* finally reaches his mature self-awareness in his choice to be simply "a man." "*I once thought/ I was Italian/...*" in the end "*I've simply chosen /with no more doubts/ to be a man*" (The Doubt). The poet will never be able to answers the many existential question he faces, but the hope still endures that around the corner he may find one day what will give meaning to it all, "*...a sudden intuition / that will swell the sense/ of my existence*" (After All).

I hope this brief introduction helps the reader to appreciate Bastianutti's poetry, which goes beyond the written space for its evocative intensity and multiple meanings.

Notes by the Author

A great number of the poems included in this collection have already been published in literary magazines and journals in both the Americas and in Europe. Some have been awarded prizes. Most are in the original English. A few have been translated in Italian and/or Spanish by the author.

For a complete list, see the Appendix on p. 153.

Contents

I.   THE BLOODY THORN

II. LOVE AFTER DUSK

III. THE ANTEVASIN

IV. SCATTERED VERSES

I may not have gone where I intended to go, but I think I have ended up where I needed to be.
Douglas Adams, *The Long Dark Tea-Time of the Soul*

I. The Bloody Thorn

The Gift

The serpent coiled

around our apple tree

and offered us

the word

For Just a While

The morning woke me
from the sequel
of my usual nightly mare
four corners of wars, depths of despair,
aid to famine and famine to AIDS
promises and threats, carrots and clubs
drunken gods playing chess on our backs
killing to save and saving the killers
of democracy and freedom
dead words draped on gun barrels
patriotism wed to terrorism
even climate is terror stricken

It's a world where
the truth will make you
a revolutionary
if the king's new clothes
are lies

Will someone help me find the shadow

of the innocent child I once was

and sew it once more

to my heels with needle and thread

so I might look into

my grandchild's

sky-blue eyes

with a promise of spring

in budding trees

hope sheltered in new birds' nest

and for a while

smile away the omens

Fools Without Borders

Perhaps

we know too much

and understand too little

our world, an emanation

of the lowest common denominator

of our flaunted democracy.

Authentic inoffensive imitations

copies of copies of copies

social mimicry of imbecility

twitted to infinity

an aping of TV

tailored to a decaffeinated,

de-nicotized, depersonalized

politically correct society

where insults must not insult

and words must mean

the least possible,

we live times of

suffering and death

artfully dissimulated

a pastel-colored life

in which idiocy seeps

into its every pore

a liberated generation

not caring where it comes from

nor where it's going

We crowd

a world once more flat

with no dreams

no gods

no myths.

Janus Moons

Words

words that shape

those perfect pearly moons

in which I wrap the thoughts

I write and read to you

who surely see the truth

reflected in the lighted face

while I reflect

upon the darker hidden face

and wonder what poison

seeps into the truth acclaimed.

But before the shadows

should stain the light

before I should lose the echo

of my voice in this ever-spreading

desert of our minds

before Gadarene-like

we should rush into a void

of our own making

I'll rip to shreds the mask

of words so well conceived

I'll stand to impeach the naked king

to say I see the evil in men's eyes

and smell the sulphur in their breath

I'll call out the false sirens in the straits

spinning webs round spineless men

who torture innocence to death

I'll scorn in pity the great kermesse

where man must be amused

if he's to give to those in need

and I'll roar my outrage

at hordes of onanists

celebrating the newest fad

of self-expression

In this world of

lying experts

man has never been

more alone and empty

and I won't go quietly

into the night.

Juggernaut

Man proposes

        and god disposes

    or is it the other way

around?

        i-Pods wafer-thin

melt in your ears

        not in your mouth

multitasking super phones

        let you

walk

    and talk

      see

       and choose

          give and

           take

    with your fingers

        all remotely human-like

borg-like fused

in single-minded mindlessness where

        all resistance's futile.

Yet now

    and then I'm nudged

        by fuzzy horns of doubt

... what if we're dumbing down

while god-like fingers fiddle

      a fail-safe system

         of control...

Future Perfect

We are taught to compute

not to think

to use Kama Sutra manuals

not to love

to buy globally

not to be individually

to move constantly toward

the new and improved

even if it's only skin-deep

to sweat for a tonic body

and boast an atonic mind

to trust in progress

at the hands of souls

bereft of humanity.

We are becoming

super specialized

with values weighed

in money

with little history

brilliantly self-centred

miserly uncouth.

We already clone sheep

we might even clone humans,

will our very souls be next?

Fahrenheit 451°

Where they burn books, so too will they in the end

burn human beings. (Heinrich Heine, *"Almansor"*, 1821)

Across the ages fires

have been burning

from Alexandria and Constantinople

to Cordoba and Cluny

Berlin Zaragoza Sarajevo

and even Washington

in the steady rising smoke

of book burning

a black hole

of the gathering night

When a book burns

man's very soul

is murdered

The Last to Die

She gentles the general's pride

a chestful of gleaming crosses

and in a trance-like gaze

she sees how many living died

to earn them

Her feverish lids rise up

to translucent stones

trembling in their sockets, eyelashes

batting loudly to the ripping

silent screams of men

whose eyes unseeing now for scenes they saw

deftly pick the lock to her awareness

She dreams a day when waves

of dying men will not give birth

to a brave new world of fodder-men

as women pay the price of birthing

in sweatered and shawled vigils.

Reality is not reversible

and more ghosts than living

crowd beneath the eaves

Night and day she scans

the world's edge

for Ariadne's saving thread

to end the endless craving

of the Minotaur in us

By the Time...

By the time you read these lines
I left you
I'll be long gone

It seems forever
that I loved you
and there was a time
you cherished me
and we were truly one
I gave myself to you without reserve
I housed you in me, on me, and of me
I warmed your home and bed
I cooked your meals and steamed your bath
granted all my gifts to you
let you climb me and carve me
I let you fashion me
to your changing tastes
I gave you shade and shelter

I even let your grafting whims

bare my virgin self away

I stripped myself naked

then I robed myself in rainbows

for your pleasure

But then you filled my home

with smoke and other toxins,

yet even in my distress

I hoped you'd change ... in vain

Your careless wasteful ways

have nearly killed me,

no more can I forgive

or understand,

our natures too at odds

Unless you change

I'll not welcome you

in my life.

Your Humble Tree

Stone Books

Row upon row of sold, demolished houses
    scars where families once lived
a fleeting mental map of homes,
      shops and schools now gone
          a lifetime wiped out
footprints of vanished skylines
displaced people who have lost
        their shadows
a vacant space with only posts
of street names
      irrelevant now remain

A world of rubble ours, not ruins
    memories wiped clean
    by bulldozers

    Without stone books to read our past,
    we'll find ourselves on Acheron's shore

with not a coin in hand

for Charon's boat.

Dies Irae

your pride and arrogance

have stripped

the earth beneath your feet

the sky above your head

even your vaunted science

cannot undo the damage done.

Pretexts and delays

have shown you false

your crocodile tears

no longer touch me.

I will consume your beaches

with ever higher waves

with cyclones eyes I'll search you out

on land and sea

Beware dies irae

the horizon's bare

there's no Ark in sight.

Monkeys

Will you see, my brother,

the lights dimming

for every tortured cry

for every sinner fried?

Will you hear

the armies of the night, my sister,

strike out to make you safe,

or hear the crying of the starving

that keep you fed,

and the groaning of the stoned

that make you feel so smug?

Will you raise your voice, my brothers,

as the lies turn to quicksand

under your feet,

as fear spins a web

around your very eyes,

as those you honour

speak falsely in your name?

What price

A snow-white conscience?

Take your hands away

and cover up no more

for the evil-doer monkey,

your fourth brother.

Crystal Birds

After dragging Domina Nocturna

up the vernal equinoctial cusp

the sun rakes dreamy gilded fingernails

down sloping hills across grainy chocolate

beaches and in preterit lines every Advent

will move across from a sunset-glossed

iron-rich green sea

with a sky above pregnant

with saints and angels blowing

slender heralds' trumpets

Yet blindly on the shore

we peer each night into the silent

scalloped pearl of the fog-shrouded sea

and we gather all but fragments

of vessels shattered at Creation

bearing witness to a game of seduction

as our masterminded god

keeps teasing us to death

No deliverer

no message

just an aggregate of single moments

with a promise of nirvana now

on the wing of crystal birds

flying up the web

of nose hair at the tip

of a rolled up Franklin bill

Comanche Territory

Do you remember
the windswept street
where I tried to corner your attention
for a dime
and all you heard was music
from the iPod in your ears

And how could you expect to notice me
thumbing for a ride
in the storm
as you passed armoured-plated
in your Hummer

And I can see how
my freezing hooded-self
could go unseen
the night you knocked me down
as you ploughed through me

wearing phone and stylish shades

Why should you recall my face
-one of many-
the day we helped to push
your limousine
from the snow drift
so you could go pump iron
in the gym

I grant,
you briefly noticed me one day
while on the phone in your SUV
as you sealed another deal
and ran distracted
over me.

Now I'm dead
with none to cry me

an accident declared

-I'm gone-

please do forgive the trouble.

Romancing the Stone

The dive had been long and deep
searching for that fleeting pin of light
the answer to the same silent question
in the near death of a coal-dark night
floating lifeless like seaweed
in the nirvanic numbness
of blessed oblivion

The agony of the slow foggy ascent
the bruised starving self surfacing
in shudders of aching consciousness
waking from a seeming timeless
cryogenic sleep in shallow gasps
and rising timid heartbeats

But again the lightless eyes crave
the cooked stone floating in the spoon
a promise-filled syringe

the hunger for absolute void

in a mind swept clean

The shaky hand eager on the plunger now

foggy eyes scan a pulsing vein

and the needle bites into the cursing blood

trading all for utter nothingness

floating in a womb

of lethal fluid

the mind a dry desert dune

sucking all thought

gone all pain

grief

    guilt

        shame

           desire

I've seen...

I've seen street corners and lanes
littered with human dregs
oh yeah

I've seen the ancient pride
of first nation
bent over
picking butts to stitch
them whole for trade
oh yeah

I've seen the mindless smile
of an ageless angel
his hair soaring with songbirds
skipping and fearlessly flying
into the rush of cars
oh yeah

I've seen the toothless grin

of a sixty-plus girl on wheels

trade a mouthful of pleasure

for a spoonful of slop

oh yeah

I've seen a legless shell

of a man fight a crow

and a mangy teary-eyed cat

over a scrap of mouldy bread

in the lane

oh yeah

I've seen a numb shivering

slip of a girl

desperate

searching for nirvana

looking for a clean track

in a darkened filthy doorway

oh yeah

I've tried to see

into eyes without sin

of the child they once were

but I swear

all I've seen

all I could see

was the ravaged face of god

I believe

oh yeah...

Noah's Ark

... it ferries a motley group of pilgrims

the activist who lost his ideals

trying to save a starving free-base whore

the truth-seeker who sold his integrity

to his drug-feeding crimes

the poet whose soul was beaten

by the moral guardians of his town...

a ship of fools whose life was crushed

in a single second

of love, hate, or plain indifference

Mother Mary full of Grace

...no more

you birthed in a plastic bag

and left it to be found

a dust-devil now you float in and out

gently calling out Grace

as you squeeze a tattered rag doll

to your naked shrivelled breast

in fear you fled Rio's favelas'
death squads with sister Maria
only to lose her along
with your mind
to angels of another kind
in Vancouver's own favelas

Weaving "Rockhead" Jimmy, you
skip down the lane shadowboxing
memories of a caring father's
drunken punches as you chase off
dragons in your private
Twilight Zone

Still straight and lean at eighty
Captain Pender, you lost your honour
to your penchant for the stone
you deadeye now a fading point

a tear swelling behind

your trademark monocle

as you yarn your days of gore and glory

through a dusting-stained moustache

Susy "Sassypants", you go weaving

every night with "Aunt Nora"

supporting your "Charlie"

buffing when you can

chicken scratching when you can't

but you're bugged more than ever

when you poke out

from the dark side of the moon

Cora, humble native woman,

you trailed from distant prairies

the bag-bride your daughter had become

here in Lotus Land where

now your strength soaks up

the darkness in your child's life

and to others

you're a shadow-storing sanctuary

in their lonely journey into the night

Der Müde Tod *(Weary Death)*

Rejoice

it is time for the black flower

of civilization to bloom

born of the macerated bones

of you and me

no longer able to measure the night

by calling out to each other

in the cacophony

of the cluttered ocean

of eternity

We have become

chthonic more than nomads

with no ossified callus

on which to anchor our soul

where time accelerates out of control

putting our future out of reach

of our children

The hard-earned freedoms

we now so cherish

have emasculated us

more than we ever were

by our shackles

The Pale Horse is weary

and has given up competing

with man's pre-eminence in his field.

Only homo sapiens

can consciously dream his own demise

with only a chosen few

divinely saved

But surely

these world-engulfing visions

of our nihilistic seed

will lay dormant

at least until tomorrow

Nobody

Hopeless we try to follow Ariadne's thread
twisting around in the labyrinth
of our good intentions
false starts
and dead ends

We have dismissed Laocoön and God
for their unwelcomed omens
and now a hidden web entraps the world
where nothing more is innocent

Hunger-grasping Tantalus
half-eaten apples thrown out by spoiled
lacquered fingers clipping coupon bonds
dishpan hands cutting discount coupons
cities consumed by flames
as others rise blind
to their last drunken dawn

A world where the haven of your home

quick turns to mortal quicksand,

from barrier against a foe

the river ends up barring your flight,

and the safety of a trench

is your tomb just as sure.

To survive in today's Cyclops's cave

we must be Nobody,

and we are closer than we think

to such a day

as even barcodes

slowly surface

       upon our face

Sixteen Pieces

It's a game, a party game we play
by touch and sound
with sixteen heavy pieces
silky smooth and polished steel
fitting parts together blindly
in fluid clicking sounds
but in the end we fail the test

Then, eyes fast shut
with practiced hand our host
in sixty seconds smoothly fits
the sixteen pieces,
stands and holds aloft the symbol
of the weak and desperate masses
against the indifferent strong
-a Kalashnikov-

Six Milliseconds on August 6th

2:45 am

the Raven rises in the translucent dawn

from the Pacific Tinian Island

with Little Boy's Dark Dream

swathed in the New Gospel

A sunny August day six hour flight away

babies nursing at the breast

trams clanging past

stray dogs barking at the sun

bird trees singing

old men pushing carts of wares

weaving bicycles in and out

garden flowers waking

a couple's tender hug

in the land of the rising sun

then...

sun-silence for six eternal milliseconds

the sudden blinding roaring light

of a pale Virgin rising in the east

head shoulders and breasts

down to her maidenhead

hovering at the horizon

the roaring of the sun stops

followed by a thunder

as the booming sound-shadow

from the Virgin's giant halo

hammers down

in a rushing breath of fire

a shimmering faint-green glow

a pulsing gale-wind wake

of slow or instant death

The sun is hushed now

the rivers of blood turned to vapour

the drumming of hearts

forever silenced

mere wall-shadows now

the few still standing

In a single flash of understanding

the pale Virgin delivered us

to the Dark Dream

of a world just six milliseconds

after man became god

Tombs and Flowers

Man dangling over the void/ from his spider's slender thread/ mends the tears by raising tombs

Giuseppe Ungaretti

A simple wooden horse

brought down Troy

the impregnable

A low-rank dagger

found the chink

in the armoured arrogance

of Paolo Uccello's knights

A simple silent sapping

crumbled San Giminiano's

soaring pride

The festive Titanic boldly

ploughed the shadows of the night

toward a fateful point

of the nautical chart ordained

by the Mariposa Effect

Twins of steel and glass built

to defy the heavens

in flaunting extension

of San Giminiano

stand no more

The enduring flower grows

over our fragile tombs.

The wind never comes down,/ it stays here among the towers,/ in the long heights,/ that one day will fall,/destroyed, crushed/ by their own self-importance.

Rafaél Alberti, New York 1982

Wreck Beach

I climbed down the sheer cliffs
shedding step by step the labels
that defined me.

It was early morning dawn when I reached
the pristine tongue of sand as the sun
hissed up and hung to fade the stars
then float and whelm it all
with its reviving light
to the gentle fluting gurgle
of the surf upon the shore

The brine-dense air was salmon-pink
and as hours without shape lapsed
gently unheeded
the sun's lidless eye roused
drowsy flies to life
as eagles screwed the sky

the emerald sea barked up a seal

and a great blue heron priested its way

along the shore with studied care

to a woodpecker's jazzed tattoo.

Time wore on as I shared the magic

of how we wear with ease

our naked skin.

As the setting sun strobed through the trees

and geese merged in a graceful fly-past

a euphony of sounds and voices held me

in a magic moment of melisma

a salute to the Sun

at Vancouver's

secret jewel.

II.   Love after dusk

Scar

Fill my life

with all of you

raise me

from all that's foul

wash the sting of evil seen

from my eyes

carve me

with your desire

that I might feel

the constant

scar of love

Silences

I stood in the lee

of women's ancient silence

eternally destined to be delivered

of sons for new Troys

and to gather,

wise and weary

their clay-footed fathers.

The Shape of Wind

I am the wind

that enfolds you

you the core

that shapes me

and

love has sealed

the light

between us

Penelope

She comes out to see the waning moon
and with parted lips catches the first sun
which perfuses a renewed fever
on all things live
and the excited calls and warbles signal
another night safely ferried to the other shore.

A giddy golden morning,
the sun an eye scorching the sky
the hour when memories thread lightly
like soft fireflies among the folds
of an idle mind.

The ache still sleeps now, but if the memories
should come in focus and stir
maybe modesty shall cease to anguish her.
Now – she reflects – you're more
than ever alone

and leave all behind as a fruit the branch.

No garden or branch where you can rest

nor song to offer nor wings to dream with

now that you only live off the remains.

These the hours when she ponders

the mystery of what the moon does to the sea

and why at times silence is still

and at others it deafens.

All seems to be key to another mystery

never to the mystery itself.

But perhaps the mystery is in her

within this tiny frail woman

her beauty as fine as her bones now

thin as the edge of a blade.

She has been moving

for such a long time already

inside her own void and yet it follows

her like a shadow–

her whole life she's dragged her cage

from one end of this zoo to the other.

And yet now, who knows what door

she has opened for her mind begins

to flush out memories concealed

in snail-like recesses of her mind.

She sees herself young once more

flying on the water's edge, her body a sheen of sea

blithe swallow, burnished dolphin

rising from the sea in a spray of diamonds

her sepia-black hair, shimmery her taut skin.

And she struggles to recall the last time

she trusted the touch of a male hand

– her father's –

the same that later handed her

over to another.

How few the steps

that brought her from love to fear

from the joy of being to the certainty

of belonging

from the desire to discover

to a life of obedience

to holding one's tongue, to suffering

to being fearfully faithful

like an eternal Penelope.

From that instant she had felt like

this island that tumbles to the sea

in ancient lava flows

wounds never healed

tentacles craving to possess

victim of explosive violence.

And the sea all around

as if to keep it from escaping

pressing on all sides.

Never again did she feel

like wading into that menacing sea

never more did she wish to undress

to be enfolded and possessed by it.

And yet how often during the first years
she shared whispers with other brides
about what there might be round the Cape
what the world was like beyond the sea.

Of that period of hunger and poverty
she recalls the soup of stones she had made
sea stones covered with tender
and tasty algac
and the sleepless nights she spent pregnant
tending to the birthing of a lamb
breast-feeding while curing warm ricotta
which she would later crib into frails
and late at night feel herself laid bare
and groped by grimy hands
that earlier had milked the sheep
with the same sense of possession.

Now she hears the sheep's bells

sound across the valley:

soon new lambs will be born

while women like herself

– dreadfully unhappy women

mortified in every crease of flesh and soul –

return now unburdened

with no regrets from the graveyard

where their shepherd

sleeps.

GiuDi

It is you who stops me

from worshipping the past

to the point of encroaching

upon our present

it is I who helps you

see that your body

though time worn

enfolds eternal youth

-your very soul-

and we help each other

avoid the constipation

of mind and spirit

by savouring the melodrama

of a biblical god betrayed

by his favourite winged

angel of light

and then by his very own brood
–our progenitors.

Ah, all these inscrutable divine errors
just to avoid dying of boredom
perfect and eternal.

Woman

Your gentle smile

able to uncover the nugget of pain

concealed deep in our happiness

the kindness of your look

able to reel in the fish of shame

in our sea of glory

the lightness of your words that slowly

peel away in ever-rising spiral

the slough of pride

we men wear...

                  Woman

To You

To lie on desert's brow
over warm hypnotic valleys
to chance the cooling rest
of rare oasis
and there to conjure up
the softness of your glen
the firmness of your dunes
to hear once more the sighs
of desert winds
and watch the rising sun
dissolve the stars
to relive our life
when we were small
the world so vast
and love so innocent

Lightly

How often have I sensed them light
as a flutter enfold my thoughts

How often have I felt their strength
as I was about to fold

How often with death in my heart
have they rallied me

How often in so many ways and plights
have your hands
loved me

Jalousie

I sit

at sand dunes' edge

casting love upon you

as my eyes trail

the ribbons

of moon

coiling your forms

through jalousies

the heaving white swells

the sensuous dip of your throat

in the shadow of your face

the silvery fascia winding

round the rising hip I trace

with fevered fingers

The pounding blood now

surges through our veins

our forms tightly enlaced

by moon rivers

flush as if

in a sudden

Apollonian noon

Barn Swallows

Like a cabbalist he tries in vain
to understand the tessitura of their love
to unfold their very own Mandala.

She ghost feathers his sleeping moments
he vamps insatiably her wakeful time
their dialogues in chromatic undertones
each searching the meager sharp sliver
of time to call their own, yet fearful
of shutting out the other.

He wears out evenings as pale as souls
fencing doubts under the cowl of her enigma
while a sharp sickle of moon rises,
flashing a scuttle of shadows across
the bonelight of his mind.

Has she found a branching of time

as if with a dowser's wand

where he's not able to follow?

Has she locked herself in her head,

this wintering sparrow he holds in his hand,

who speaks not words

but words in halos of meaning

like barn-swallow's souls rising

to mine and hollow out a region of light

in the blindness of his mind?

The Shape of Absence

Her gone, I recreate her running
my fingers
in the hollow of her head on the pillow
I caress her in the dresses
that recall her body

I inhale her scent in the towel
that tightly breathed around her hips
I seek her on the sill
that pressed her breasts

on the sofa where she yielded
to reveries
in the sun-fresh washing,
in her shampoo or in the kitchen

in her modesty
when she passes from lover to woman

in the dense scent of desire

that spreads out like a secret

in the perfume of the night

dark veil that envelops her

sated and languid she-cat

And it's this shadow of woman

that has burrowed deep in my soul

a shadow sealed in a castle of shadows

congeries of shadow that bend

in a melancholic smile.

And the sea speaks even now

of autumn.

You

I spy the sudden quiver
beneath the filly's coat
and I feel you

I bite into the velvet
of a freshly plucked peach
and I taste you

I listen to the sweet interlace
of birds at first light
and I hear you

I sink my fingers
in the warm fur of a cat
and I lose myself in you

I gently lift the hem
of a sleepy sea

and I see you

I drain the ruby red
of a rare vintage
and I delight in you

I spy the peeking moon
over the ridge of a knoll
and I grow bright with you

I lay my gaze
next to yours and I sense you
thinking of me

A Spark

Words are dangerous,
and for years
words was all they had
rattling against the walls
of their marriage
she laid awake the nights
secretly her husband
awake with her
and she often felt that life
had to be elsewhere

How long she had spied
with eucharistic patience
for him to show a spark of life
yet he barely ever managed
the intelligent look
of a sloth

Today she has bettered

the fourth Horseman

not knowing or caring

if she would reach the end alive

at sixty-five

She has won another day

her own

and she'll spend it

in new places

new faces

new feelings

forging a new life

alone

A Soul's Sweat

Sempre più lenta l'alba

e rapido il tramonto

Like bees from their hive

memories swarm out of me

and the wind whistles aches

through my bones

as I run to stay my death

the old skin left behind

The liquid shadow I once was

a raven cat sliding through shards

of moonrays breaking up

my nights, in a maze of carping eyes

their every breath a sour taste of gossip

All the while a ceaseless longing

clutched my heart

an ache buried

deep in my dreams

a secret self whose shadow I chased

and found at last

Like a sleepwalker over the abyss

I plunged my loneliness

into the sunstream of your love

and we laid down throbbing

to the rhythm of an ancient pulse

in the whispering stillness

just before a new dawn

I Want...

I want to slow the streak of stars
the lunar flashing curve
in the night sky
    my love
I want the world to wake a little later
each morning
the tides to ebb a little slower
the sun to sleep a little longer
the fields to patiently wait
the harvest moon delayed
the rivers to check their flow
    my love
their waters stretching out
and lazily rolling over the lip
never quite falling
I want yesterday today and tomorrow
to blur into a never-ending moment
as I sit across from you

    my love

and see the woman

into which all women blur

and know you

by the look that kills

the caress that heals

the touch that cares

the kiss that loves

    my love

Above the Horizon

In ceaseless thirst
the desert dances on thorns
of love
shadows upon shadows
entwining flesh
over enfolding flesh

She lets him take her like the night
swallows the sun in the lunar
tidal heartbeat
with his sky planted in her body
she howls like the moon melting
into the sea
a lashing whip
a swirl of colours
on its fevered tip

Becalmed

she brings him in

whispering his name

as he reads forgotten messages

on her veined wrists

To Parse

One Spring

when February borrows

 days from March

and the wind swallows up the rain

as a gospel of frogs

tunes up in the fenlands,

I'd like to parse and praise

the Sun

that warms our earth

the Rains

that quench its thirst

the Winds

that carry seeds from far off lands

the Clouds

that crowd the stage above

the Light and Shadows

and the many Colours of our skin

the rich and varied Scents of this earth

and of the seas that bind her

I'd like to praise and parse

its Bounty

and the Love

for Beauty and Justice

that hold us fast

to this spinning orb

Enigma

She administers her silence like no other,
a tongue she has spoken
for thousands of years

In front of her
he often feels like
a well-lubricated ghost,
possessing her, yet not her silent thoughts,
wondering how she populates the desert
of her silence when she feels his seed
by him forgotten,
and what she smiles at
when she looks right past him

She stares at him with a mixture
of boredom, wisdom, and weariness.
Her gaze is neither elusive nor sustained
neither inquisitive nor indifferent:

how many generations of women
were needed to achieve that gaze
as penetrating as a steel blade
born from a long genetic memory
of untold lives spent as prey
in dark holds of ships, her thighs bloody
among burning ruins and bodies,
weaving and unweaving her cloth
across endless winters

How often has he sensed the presence
of thousands upon thousands of them
behind this woman's steady presence
in every corner of his life

He envies her free love
a love not prize-driven
for she's as pure as a theorem
as dense as a black star

Deep down he sees her armed

with all the weapons god and nature

have granted woman to defend herself

Yet undaunted,

the intemperate pride bred in his blood

drives his desire to penetrate her

to become her watchmaker

to examine her in her sleep

to snatch the secret cogwheels

to uncover her between clicks

Though he often thinks

himself her lover, in the end

he must concede

he's simply her witness

God's Finger

I wait as night after
night swallows dusk
blurring all idle details
to focus on your core

More than your body your shadow
has bound me in a spell
leading me to dream
and undream myself in you
as I quarry the luminous trace
God's finger blessed you with

My eye a prism
splintered by the unquenched desire
to catch and hold yours
sensing you have a world
to tell me
wanting to pour some day

into my nights

Not lured into demented spasms
by winds of fear
blowing faint and deadly
from the future
you and I may well age
in bursts of time
but we plumb the depth
of our days not their breadth
as we lay down together
my head on the pillow
to dream you
as you'll dream me
on the flip side
just like children
for the dead
have not yet entered
our dreams

The Hand

Reaching out
man and God conceive
each other in convoluted
hierarchy

Born to life with ready traced lines
the icastic hand that speaks in silence
hand that sees and foresees in darkness
curious hand that distrusts
the world spied
hand that dreams to touch
that which we dream

self-contained the hand
in eternal struggle with itself
mano faber and *mano ludens*
in good and evil
hand that yearns for peace and plots a war

that grants life and takes it away
hand that prays and hand that deceives
that forgives and that condemns
that blesses and that cuts off other hands
hand that breaks clods and offers a breast
that counts money and runs off beads
blood-stained hand that begs for mercy
loving hand that brushes a caress
hand of a brute that kills for love
patient hand that ages weaving
and unweaving as it lies in wait

But no hand is more expressive
in its slightest fleeting gesture
in quivers light as gossamer wings
in myriad moods
of first unchecked desires
or wicked thoughts
than a woman's gentle hand.

After a Long Flight

Will it be like after a long flight

with folded wings upon themselves

to float upon the shallow waters

of our memories

to graze again the signs

of desire's ancient tides

to climb the shore

of time-bleached bones

to rummage

memory's forgotten corners

and find each other

in a sudden spray of foam?

Love after Dusk

An hour after dusk
disappears into the earth
night removes
all your details
and an ancient wind presses
against our tangled shadows

I hold your eyes
with mine knowing
nothing could be the same
again the blood blurs
my mind with a rush
of feelings grasping
at your unfinished nature
a metaphor veiled in flesh
purely in loan to me
I move in Stygian darkness
groping like an owl for a soul

to consume your elusive shadow

new and fresh each time through

the prism of my eyes

Floating

Every time I look at you
it's like the first time
so light in love we float
in clear blue waters
breathing pure sea breeze
as we walk hand in hand
in the shadow of a rainbow
the world around us
gone

II. The Antevasin

To Myself

As I write these words

to a younger me

the me I left back

there and then

yet I've always loved you

just as you were then.

I still see you bathed

in sun, while here

my own tree

casts an ever longer

shadow.

Class of '39

Too young to have hated or loved

the world that saw me born

too young to have fought

to change it

or to defend it

but old enough to have understood

that my spring was born

from the snows five-winters long

that my innocence was redeemed

by a five-year old amnesia

that with the rubble

had swept away a past as well

that had bloomed in me

yet bore no fruit

Liberty Ship

In vain the eye tries to block out
scenes still true

In vain I compute the equation
between dignity and want
in the sailor's sneering stare
at stateless children
as they grasp like mice
fresh fruit he has flung
around him on the floor

On deck I watch the muddy Mississippi
churning with hungry blacks
in the wake of spoiled foodstuffs
dumped from the "General Sturgis"
my *Liberty Ship*

Ephemeral

I caress the physical truth

of this object on my desk

once given to me in pledge

it has survived intact

a past ephemeral love

just like a star long dead

whose light still shines

though its warmth is felt

no more.

Twice Displaced

I am the world in which I walk,
displaced from my homeland
as much as from myself

Yet even now my very own past
has become a foreign land to me
where what I see and hear and feel
is no longer mine

And as the years grow heavy
the more I feel as if
I'm treading a land twice foreign

Time has displaced me
as much as distance did so long ago,
all has become once more
so alien

I wonder if

the world forgetting

by the world forgot

might indeed

be true

Beloved Albatross

Are the dead my credentials?

What was my loss worth?

Through the thick fog of time I still see

a living frontier on the move:

Germans crossing the Oder trading fears

with Lublin-fleeing Poles,

Sudetens and East Prussians drifting

from Berlin to DP camps

Slavs purging Italians

from their ancestral home

all fleeing, criss-crossing

the scorched, blood-soaked lands

of the Imperial cauldron

limping, shuffling, clutching

relics of an order forever gone

which no alchemist will ever

reassemble.

He, like so many, a DP

a euphemism coined for a non entity

his forehead, hands, and ass rubber-stamped

deloused, de-fascistified, de-communistified,

poked, probed, palpated, re-named,

classified, consigned, invoiced, re-routed, detained

ignored, uprooted, and re-planted

in virgin foreign soil.

Now and then he still strokes

half-consciously his beloved albatross

for he cannot let go

the one ghost-feather

his fingers keep brushing

    - Fiume -

He still hears her calling out to him.

Perhaps one day he'll dismiss her

but... not just yet,

as he fingers rusty locks

whose keys he's yet to find.

The Doubt...

I once thought I was
Italian
then in the slicing and carving
of time and lands
I found myself
in no-man and everyman's land
and I became
a reverse chameleon
I was black to the reds
and red to the blacks
Italian to Croats
and Croat to Italians

In doubt
they dubbed me a D.P.
and shipped me to find
the American dream
where I was called *Dago*

and *WAP*

Then

after a life of crossing borders

I returned to my "motherland"

where I was called

Doctor, Professor, Prophet

Now I've simply chosen

with no more doubts

to be a man

Dying to Live

I tried to hearse and rehearse

my life

over all these decades

crossing borders and oceans

and in the end I found myself

beached and bleached

all skin 'n bones on shaky legs

still forced to carry

my unfulfilled desires

as I live and love

over ancient mounds

of covered bones

Still Here

I've barely time to recall the almond trees

in bloom painted above me on the ceiling

before slice by slice my brain

is scanned as I slide strapped

to a gurney through a halo of probing rays

    -eyes closed-

yet I see the scene of blossomed almonds

on the ceiling of my home on the Riviera

as I stretch on the marble floor

the sun streaming through the terrace

    - eyes closed and don't move -

I see me running barefoot

in the chestnut grove below my house

a roebuck skipping from stone to stone

swinging from tree to tree

jumping off 10-foot farmed terraces

    -keep still, please. We're almost done

I'm swimming in the surf at Portofino

diving deep to lay my hands

on the sunken statue of Christ

then quickly rising to the myriad suns

dancing on the surface of the ink-blue sea

   -You may move now. We'll have the results in a few days.

I look up now and the almond trees are bare.

Time

How quickly the past becomes the past

when the wind of passing time

blows faint and deadly

when the world is meaningless and less

in its orphaned frenzy of bytes,

a fantasy of sounds

an orgy of colours

as the breach between man and woman

widens

His world happens in someone else's

hers happens within herself

she has the night in her mouth

in his he grinds a silent roll of thunder

and between her silence and his

each inhales and exhales time

shrinking the present

between a slowing past

sliding

toward a dying future

So we retreat in dreams

where the living and the dead

speak a single primal tongue

and a brazen crow flies overhead

its two black wings

combing the wind

of time

Life Spied

Still drowsy the sea is breathing

a cat's-paw in delicate shades

and far off the shrill cries

of sea swallows slicing the air

usher in a new dawn

Plunging seagulls, sudden splashes

shatter this slick swatch of sea

as if to stray our thoughts

from the dark abyss

and not feel our life spied

by death

Night Poker

Stock-still the cypress grove

guards in dark solemnity

the *ignis fatuus*

of poker-playing souls

flickering

on marble tops

their whispered laughter

slowly dying

as the night gives

its ghost away

to dawn

Time Unleashed

I've learned to live

time unscanned

I've learned to spy the space

between two actions

I've learned to feel the quiver

of a lowered eyelid

the color of a thought

disguised by words

I've learned to live the desert spaces

the discarded moments

I've learned to savour futures

mediated by a past

not yet spoiled

by a present

and thus conjugate

my life time

Aqua Mater

Water

    dawn-dew water

      water clouds

        rain water

          spring water

fresh-river water

          mountain-lake water

salty water

    of sweet tears of joy

        holy water

atoned with blood

      lachryma water

      of broken hearts

Water that runs

    to the sea

      the sea

  a seafull of water

      sea water

living water

       water alive in me

cradling me

    pulling me

      whelming me

foaming my flesh

     enfolding it

       and moulding

my primal past

    in the salty placenta

      of the sea

Musing

The bare branches are etched
against a low leaden sky:
the intrigue of life suspended
tracing the distance of a raven's flight.

The weight of my thoughts crushes
a dead branch and the splinters
shard the pure silence
of dawn

Birds and squirrels crisscross
in multi-coloured flight,
then, wavered by doubt,
they scent out
the fear.

But soon the falling snow
restores the stillness

and I resume once more

my journey.

Floaters and Moonslivers

Floaters
he calls them
but
I see moonslivers
retinal tugs he says
but I smile
I know better

For years she's chased me
casting far in front
her long black shadow
so I knew a fearful
abstract symmetry of life
was waiting
for me to trip
along the way and snatch me

She hovers now

barely in front

our shadows stretching

at our back

I see at night

floating before my eyes

her torn black veil

I catch the moonlight glint

off her polished blade

day by day she takes the measure

of my weary stride

at night

she whispers my name in shadows

upon shadows

trying to take me

the way dusk whelms the light

But I close my eyes

you see

and I see I see

now that I

understand

Figtree

fragile spider webs quiver

as they sieve

the first fleeting breaths

of winter for long-forgotten

memories

silky strands tethered

to ever fewer life posts

I shield the figtree

against the coming frost

A Life

Summer is over, the fireflies are dead

and the harvest is done

the rains hold sway now and already

I detect the subtle odour of ageing

happy and at peace

Day by day my island is shrinking

hour by hour I shift

to search the sun's last rays

as I see my shadow lengthen

dying to merge with the night

dogging me

I recall my many flights

along the levees of time

when I'd seek the sun

that cast no shadow

that impossible place

with a mere shadow of light

where to walk between the two

where in a whisper of time

I might hear the songs

of my blood wrapped in pearls

of silence

I stop now to rest

beneath the cope of that dream

so real that I still feel my soul

vibrate as the branch

still quivers for the bird

that has just lifted off.

Immortality

I thump

from time to time

on my coffin

to hear echoes

of an ever more

dubious

immortality

After All...

I find myself

ever closer to some kind of ending

my present pressed

by an overflowing past

living what feels like

a posthumous life

bereft of any analgesic cliché

to ease the growing angst

Every friend lost

marks a period of my life

and a looming loneliness

in a future shy of new surprises

and yet...I keep hoping after all

that round tomorrow soon

I might be struck by a sudden intuition

that will swell the sense

of my existence

Here's looking at you

Will his monsters come to birth

in some dark corner of his mind?

From the vantage point

of his seven decades of decanting life

into a large leaky barrel

his posthumous eyes

look at the wreckage of his ambitions

as ash to the waterline

and that will be that....

IV. SCATTERED VERSES

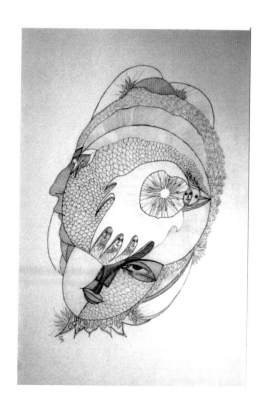

The Shepherd

(Hale-Bopp Comet 305 B.C. – 1997 A.D.)
Caltavuturo, Sicily

He must have been a thousand years old or more
the blue-eyed shepherd
his dark face lit by the bonfire
the night the comet passed
over the uplands of Trinacria.

It saw him brood in his solitude
like a gargoyle above the slumbering town
just as it had left him centuries before
– tall, his chin resting on his staff
a wolf's skin covering his shoulders
his flock gathered in the arms
of stones, thorn-bush and prickly pears
and it recognized in the enduring scene
the ever present shepherd, the very same
who has seen all the dawns of the world
stars born and die to an indifferent heaven
and the shadow of every moon glide alongside him

– the shepherd–

unaware of his own immortality, his days mere lima-bean
shells heaping in a bottomless time-worn dossel.

In the endless nights of the ages
when flitting fires like bright-lit eyes
of wolf or owl seemed to pierce his very soul,
he dreamed the chase of clouds
driven first by Phoenician gusts, Greek easterlies, then by
Arabian siroccos or Bourbon draughts and Fascist gusts
each with rains of blood and fire
tears and words, words in the name
of the one and multiple cryptic god
as hard and indifferent as a fisted hand.
And all this is but a single day
seamless, eternal as a serpent.

His always the task of silently skinning
the sheep abandoned by the fleeing wolf
while the bloodied night heralds a cold dawn
with a sun so hard his teeth rattle in his head
and he warms his hands with the warm fresh blood in

the hollow of a cliff that bursts with screeching swifts.

His head swathed in a mystified smile, a crease of silence
wounds his face, only a cold and bitter sweat between
himself and the rising wind
while he spies himself in the bedevilled eye
of the ill-temper goat that has always fed
on malefic and mysterious grasses.

He plows the morning fog with his flock
in the unchanging pagan and Christian litany
bound around a hard timeless silence
in the dull stillness of his own calloused thoughts
of memories, lingering as a winter illness
with the muscles of his mind's eye that have always
merged the elements and the seasons in atavic harmony
to keep the flux of time in a self-contained existence of
transhumance, milking and shepherding.

And so today like every yesterday the sheep flock
to the fields of salt-siren sighing in the wind
sundry melodies until their forms dissolve
licked clean by glares and rainfalls

and tongued by oxen, goats and rams.

The shepherd's every instant is but a moment
of ancient times already ravaged, there is no other time.
At night he keeps watch with one eye
and feigns death with the other
while behind his eyelids flits a dream
a dream of whispers, hints of screams
wails of the flesh, stifled moans down there
in the narrow lanes of the village, of cries
that rise up the mountain's narrow gorge.

He dreams ageless fevers of desire, and shy
he suffers jeremiads, a timeless primal lore
from Hellenic ancestors and he remains
spellbound with his eyes shut tight
his mouth pressed in emblematic Homeric crease
with gestures charged with mythic tragedy
of timeless savage strength repressed.
He dreams of myths that fly in the night
and he casts glances at the pitiful females
coming to bring him creature comforts
hapless women, venal females, women-myth

who appear out of the fog amid bleating sheep
the scent of female, of bird-women
with eager eye and voice of turtledove in love
chanting ancient songs in the dark of night
the horse-women with the smile of a tiger
and of a siren, sparks of lunacy in their eyes
their hair spread over breasts and shoulders
– myths that sleep in the shelter of his cave.

Thus he dreams the woman-myth, her hands
and face scratched by lustful stares
that have grazed her for centuries
her quick eyes, her mouth slower
than her ears, that's how the shepherd dreams her
in the shadow of his mind's eye
when he brings his flock down to the pit
of the Greek theatre as ever tightly bound
within the ruins of its timeless silence.

He dreams of sharing his meal with her
the woman-myth with the face of all the women
never born and to be yet born.
He recalls lighting the fire in the proscenium

and the crackling of twigs and dried dung
echoes from the very last row of the theatre.

He throws mushrooms and sausages on the embers and
with his finger he follows the last ray of the sun
tracing the names of patricians carved on the seats
ancient and alien syllables of dead men.

He eats now sitting next to the woman-myth
in the perfect acoustics of the age-encrusted bowl
and two hundred pairs of dead ears are cocked
listening to their chewing that reaches intact
each and every seat, and is then echoed in the pit
and it's as if all those ancestral ghosts
had come back to life
to share his meal.

With wine he puts out the fire
the hissing spreads all round
and together with the conjured dead
he too disappears in the fog of his dream
as one bleat echoes another

Leather Dialogues

(To Simon Brugnone, Cefalù 2003)

An abstract idea his cobbler shop

nailed on two planks, leeward

in the shelter of silence

along the steps of Paramura

that wind down to Rionero

between damp courtyards of ochre tufa

worn down by briny air, filigreed with lichen

old Simon toils away

with skiving knife wax twine and resin

and furtively scans passersby

in search of the Word

A solitary iconoclast

      - u scarparu -

white six-day old stubble

a bitter smile of nails

a St. Elmo's fire

matching the arrhythmia

of his hammer

His motions are paced, confident

as if performed for a thousand years

not work but life itself

and so too his words

clear powerful articulate

like his hammer

Alone at day's end

in that hour that drifts

by stealth into darkness

a pearl of silence grows

around a grain of sand

golden embryo of assured renewal

that frees him from chains and cages

free to measure himself with new spaces

with no need to trade freedom for security

His has always been a Ionic seduction

a life of justice and freedom in constant dialogue

with small sacred images tacked on the walls

- Gramsci Falcone Borsellino -

incensed by wax, glue, black polish and sweat

It's getting late

the sun has already dipped

beneath the hem of the sea

Tired now, he puts out the light

shuts the door and murmurs words

read who knows where

-It's late, every day more late-

Bianca

The horrors her eyes had seen across

those orphaned years across

two wars and more across

borders seas and oceans across

peoples' tongues and mores

all she endured with grace and dignity

though her gentle soul

was scarred forever

She repaired

to more congenial worlds in old and new

books and with pen in hand

she forged tenuous bridges

to her dispersed world

She was and is for me

the absolute expression

of a lost age

with that sense of noblesse

of views and feelings

honed by a moral integrity

whose vague scent

is all we have left

Never again will I rest

my trusting hand

on her shoulder as she swam me

out to sea

a fresh warm bread her kisses

a safe cove her embrace

a bosky serenity her voice

her thoughts pure and guiless

Yet still now

I draw comfort

from the memory of her hands

Luigi

I never knew if we laughed at you or with you

now I know what you most valued

was a smile to lighten our progress

laughter to banish despair from our eyes

if only for a while

and yet how often you shut yourself off

in the stubborn silence of a gentle

wounded soul, a fleeting flash

of sadness in your eyes

the chagrin of seeing your simplicity

misjudged by us

A war left you orphan of a childhood

with grownup cares

orphaned of love and affection

you sought all your life

a man of the world yet so vulnerable

clever and wise though unschooled

as only those guided by love can be

you could be the life of the party

yet in the many fateful moments of our life

you found the dignity and the courage

to pilot us safely across wars and oceans

hand in hand with mamma

You who felt such pride in your children

continue to live in our memories

in your unfeigned smile

your indulgent acceptance

of human frailties

your constant effort to banish

pride and umbrage from our hearts

You left us surrounded by the love

you had sown and us knowing

who you were in truth

APPENDIX

POEMS PUBLISHED IN ANTHOLOGIES, ACTS OF CONGRESSES, AND LITERARY JOURNALS

1. "Ossa", "Come sarà?", "Cicatrice", "Scar", "Silenzi", "Una vita", in *Strange Peregrinations: Italian Canadian Literary Landscapes*", The Frank Iacobucci Centre for Italian Canadian Studies, 2007, pp. 159-161.
2. "Juggernaut" in *The Toronto Quarterly*, n. 4, September 2009.
3. "The Shepherd" in *Feile-Festa: The Literary Arts Journal of the Mediterranean Celtic Cultural Association* (New York), Fall 2009.
4. "Enigma" 2° Prize ($200) Drummond Poetry Contest 2009; read at the Classic Theatre in Cobalt, Ont. March 27, 2009; published in *Expressions* 2009 and launched at the *Spring Pulse Poetry Festival 2009*.
5. Interview on the CBC *West by North-West* for my Prize-winning book of poetry "For a Fistful of Soil", 2009.
6. "A Burning Question" ($50) published in *Expressions 2009*.
7. "Just for a While", published in *Expressions* 2009.
8. "Wreck Beach", published in *Expressions* 2009.
9. "Imposte/Jalousie", Antologia Poetica "Poesia Romantica" directed by ESTRO-VERSO, The Italian Association of Authors, Artists, and Editors.
10. "Barn Swallows", 1st Prize ($300) in 2010 Drummond Poetry contest, published in *Expressions 2010*.

11. Interview "Incontro con il poeta", *L'Amico d'Italia*, n.127, January 2010.
12. "The Forester" in *Celebrating Poets Over 70*, McMaster University, 2010, p. 46.
13. "Amado Albatros", "Enigma", "Lunas de Jano", in *Poesìa del Encuentro: Antologìa del VII Encuentro Internacional de Escritores*, Costa Rica, 2010, pp. 167-70.
14. An Invited Reading of my poetry at an International Symposium for the "Settimana della Lingua Italiana" in Toronto, October 22-23, 2010.
15. "Lineamenti per una mia prassi poetica" in *Rivista di Studi Italiani*, Anno XXIX, n. 1, giugno 2011, pp. 279-287 (poems included: "Amato albatro", "Ossa", "Rondine", "Arcano" , "Un poker notturno", "Janus Moons", "Tombs and Flowers".)
16. "Dying to Live", "To Parse", "Twice Displaced", "Time" in *Italian Canadiana*, n. 23, Fall 2009, pp. 109-116.
17. "Dying to Live", "To Parse", "Twice Displaced", "Time" in *Bibliosofia2. n.104-110*, September 2010.
18. "Beloved Albatross", *FEILE-FESTA*, Spring 1011.
19. "Un poker notturno", *L'Amico d'Italia*, 132, luglio 2011, p. 35.
20. "El serrallo", *Isla Negra*, 7/356, 2013 (Buenos Aires, Argentina)
21. "Leather Dialogues", *Feile-Festa 2013* (New York).
22. "Golondrina", *Isla Negra*, 9/359, 2013
23. "Una vida" , *Isla Negra*, 9/361, 2013
24. "I've Seen", *The Well House*, 3 (Indiana Univ.), 27 November, 2013.

25. "Above the Horizon", *The Well House*, 4 (Indiana Univ.) 27 November 2013.
26. "The Last to Die", *The Well House*, 4 (Indiana Univ.) December 2013.
27. "Voices of Italian Poetry of the 20th and 21st Century", Readings at the Vancouver Italian Cultural Institute, Dec. 6, 2012 and Jan. 22, 2013 (I was one of the poets read).
28. "I've seen...", "Comanche Territory", "Time", "You", "The Last to Die", "To You", "Above the Horizon", "A Soul's Sweat", at *Vancouver Books & Biscotti*, June 17, 2014.
29. "Enigma", *Isla Negra*,10/385, 2014, p. 22.

ABOUT THE AUTHOR

Diego Bastianutti was born in Italy, completed his studies at the University of Toronto, and was a professor at Queen's University (1970-96). Since his retirement he counts among his publications, *A Major Selection of the Poetry of Giuseppe Ungaretti*, in 1997, winner of the "1998 John Glassco Prize"; his third poetry collection, *For a Fistful of Soil / Per un pugno di terra*, was awarded the 2008 *International Literary Prize Scritture di frontiera*. His prize-winning poems and short stories have been featured in various literary journals and anthologies in the Americas and in Europe. Currently he is a Canadian correspondent for an Italian cultural magazine in San José, Costa Rica. He resides in Burnaby, BC with his wife. He is the happy father of two daughters and four grandchildren plus two. He delights in travelling with his wife.

Made in the USA
Charleston, SC
23 December 2014